IMAGES
of England

WEST DERBY
AND
NORRIS GREEN

Drinking fountain, West Derby village, 1932. The fountain was a gift from Richard R. Meade-King, who lived at 'Broomfield'. The inscription reads, 'Water is best'.

IMAGES
of England

WEST DERBY
AND
NORRIS GREEN

Compiled by
Kay Parrott

TEMPUS

Mab Lane, *c.* 1897. This old farmhouse was once the residence of the Chantrells.

First published 1996
Reprinted 2001 and 2004

Tempus Publishing Limited
The Mill, Brimscombe Port,
Stroud, Gloucestershire, GL5 2QG
www.tempus-publishing.com

British Library Cataloguing in Publication Data.
A catalogue record for this book is available from the British Library.

ISBN 0 7524 0682 5

Typesetting and origination by Tempus Publishing Limited.
Printed in Great Britain by Midway Colour Print, Wiltshire.

Contents

Bennison's Map of the town and port of Liverpool, 1835. Scale $6\frac{1}{4}$" = 1 mile. This section covers West Derby village.

Introduction

The majority of photographs in this book are of West Derby and Norris Green although a few of Gillmoss, Croxteth and Cantril Farm have been included. The area covered is roughly bounded by the East Lancashire Road to the north, the present boundary of the City of Liverpool to the east, Yew Tree Lane, Honey's Green Lane and Alder Road to the south, and Queens Drive to the west. West Derby and Norris Green make an interesting contrast. The former is long established and still has a recognisable village centre, with a parish church, a mixture of houses of different dates and types, local shops and a large country house. The latter is a large estate, planned and built by Liverpool Corporation in the 1920s, in response to a housing crisis after the First World War.

West Derby is mentioned in the *Domesday Book* and at that time was more important than Liverpool, then just a small fishing village on the banks of the River Mersey. However as early as the thirteenth century West Derby declined in relative importance as Liverpool started to grow. West Derby had its own castle, situated just to the north of where St Mary's Church is now. The castle originated in Saxon times and probably stood for several hundred years. As the site of the local manor court, the area was an important legal centre, from the Middle Ages onwards. The sixteenth-century courthouse can still be seen in the centre of the village and was used to settle local land disputes as late as 1825. The first reference to a church in the village is in the fourteenth century. Today's parish church of St Mary the Virgin replaced a much older and smaller building in the 1850s.

Vestiges of West Derby's past survive. The village stocks, a cheaper alternative to prison, were repositioned early this century in what used to be the village pound. Stray sheep or cattle were kept here until their owner was able to pay a fine for their release.

In the fifteenth and sixteenth centuries West Derby was a collection of thatched cottages, clustered around the centre of the village. By the late eighteenth and early nineteenth centuries the main route through the village was Almond's Green and its continuation Town Row. The area was a quiet rural district, with a population of just 2,636. However the nineteenth century saw a huge growth in the population to over 100,000. Sixty large houses were built in West Derby for the merchants of the rapidly expanding city of Liverpool. These mansions all required servants and supplies, contributing further to the expansion of the village. In addition to the merchants' houses West Derby had its own country house and park at Croxteth Hall. This was the principal residence of the Earls of Sefton, the Molyneux family. The gates of the extensive park open in the centre of West Derby village. Despite this, the estate was largely self sufficient and connections with the village were never close.

The Norris Green estate was Liverpool Corporation's most important suburban development project in the inter-war years. House building, both in the private and public sectors, had virtually stopped during the First World War and this, coupled with a rising birth rate, meant that by 1923 there were over 20,000 applicants on the housing register. Various governments passed legislation promoting the repair and demolition of insanitary property and imposing restrictions on overcrowding.

The estate was constructed on 680 acres of primarily agricultural land acquired by the Corporation. Work began in 1926 and in the first two years 5,351 houses, out of a projected 8,000, were built. The estimated final population for the new estate was 30,000. Houses were built at densitities of 12 to 16 per acre and the population reduced from 250 per acre in the city centre to only 50 per acre. Most of the houses were built by private contractors, who each worked on different sections of the estate. The majority of the houses were the so-called non-parlour type, with one main living-room, practically no hall and a downstairs bathroom. Built in blocks of 2, 4, 6, or 8, they had no ornamentation or architectural details, although all had front and back gardens. Due to financial pressures landscaping was reduced to a minimum and to avoid monotonous rows of identical streets it was decided to group the houses in crescents, closes, squares and concentric circles, an arrangement which many new tenants found very confusing. These plain houses contrasted with those built earlier by the Corporation under different legislation, such as those on the Lark Hill estate, a number of which are also illustrated in this book.

Despite this minimalistic approach most new tenants thought that their standard of living had improved and were happy with their new homes, especially compared with previous living conditions. However the new estate had its problems. Very few of the new residents knew each other, coming from a variety of inner city locations, with mixed religious and educational backgrounds. Their tightly-knit local communities were broken up in the mass movement of people to the suburbs and many found it hard to adjust. The Corporation concentrated on building houses and in this they succeeded, but there were delays in providing amenities on the estate. The first schools were opened in 1926 in temporary, wooden buildings, but many children commuted, at the Corporation's expense, to schools outside the area. There were few shops and again people travelled to, for example, Lisburn Lane, in Tuebrook or the Great Homer Street Market, where prices were cheaper. Transport was difficult and expensive. Tramway routes stopped on the boundaries of the estate. The Corporation decided that no pubic houses would be built on the estate, although breweries got around the ban by building on the borders. Churches were not built until after the houses were completed and the tenants had moved in. For a variety of reasons – lack of amenities, increased unemployment and the high cost of transport – over forty per cent of the original tenants left before the estate was ten years old. The photographs in this book show the estate during its construction and shortly after completion.

The majority of the photographs in the volume come from collections in Liverpool Record Office, Liverpool Central Library. These are from the Photographs and Small Prints Collection, photographs taken by the City Engineers Department (reference 352 ENG) and Housing Department Photographs (reference 352 HOU). A number of additional photographs have been loaned by members of the West Derby Society.

One
West Derby Village

Church of St Mary the Virgin, West Derby village, *c*. 1890. This church was built to replace the much older West Derby chapel, situated in the centre of the village, which had its origins in the fourteenth century.

Church of St Mary the Virgin, 1942. This interior view shows the gothic design of Sir Giles Gilbert Scott. The church was built using money raised entirely by subscription and was consecrated in 1856. The old West Derby chapel was then demolished. It had originally been intended to have a peal of bells installed in the tower, but as the church was built on sandy soil, it was thought that the vibrations from the bells would damage the foundations.

West Derby village, c. 1915. This is one of a number of postcards of the area produced by the, as yet, unidentified firm of T.P. & Co. The shop on the left, at the corner of Mill Lane, belonged to William Jessop, victualler.

West Derby village, *c.* 1930. This view is looking towards Croxteth Park entrance. On the left, behind the car, are numbers 2-6 Almond's Green. These Victorian cottages were designed, in the 1880s, by Eden Nesfield, who also designed the village cross in the centre.

West Derby village, 1914. This postcard was sent to an address in Hesketh Bank, near Preston, in 1914. The cost was one halfpenny.

West Derby village, *c.* 1897. This gives a good idea of how the village centre looked at the end of the nineteenth century. The scene suggests a warm summer's afternoon. The well-dressed lady on the left has a parasol to protect her from the sun and the woman in the white bonnet

rests in the shade on the steps of the courthouse. The tram horses wait patiently for their passengers.

Yeoman's House, 1900. This house is dated 1660 and is typical of a yeoman's house of that time. It is built of sandstone although it was, for many years, whitewashed. The small, stone mullioned windows are typical of the period. The building to the left is occupied by Hooper and Simmons, coachbuilders, established *c*. 1879 (see p.17) .

Town Row, *c*. 1900. This old cottage is one of a number which stood in Town Row in the nineteenth century. It may have been constructed of large crucks of timber, which formed the basic framework of the building. The spaces between the crucks would have been filled either with wattle, daubed with mud or cob, a kind of mud concrete.

West Derby village, *c.* 1915. This postcard view was probably taken in the early morning. The two women are both cleaning their steps and the man on the ladder is attending to, what would then have been, a gas light. The licensee of the public house on the left was John Kermack and he sold beer supplied by Joseph Jones and Co. of Knotty Ash.

The Monument, *c.* 1910. The Monument, also known as the Village Cross, was designed by Eden Nesfield and given to the local community by Mrs Pemberton Heywood, of the house 'Norris Green', between 1861 and 1870. The monument marks the sight of the old chapel of St Mary the Virgin, demolished when the new church was built in the 1850s.

West Derby Courthouse, *c.* 1910. West Derby was an important legal centre from the Middle Ages onwards and the present courthouse dates from 1586. The local manor court was held here and the building was still in use as a courthouse as late as 1825. By 1921 the building had fallen into disrepair and was in danger of being demolished. However, a group of local trustees acquired the lease from the owner, Lord Salisbury, for a peppercorn rent of 2s 6d (12½p).

West Derby Courthouse, 1935. This interior view gives some idea of how the building must have looked when still in use. The courthouse also housed important local records, which were kept in the 'Town Chest'. For greater security this had a number of locks, with different keyholders, all of whom had to be present when the chest was opened.

Village stocks. The stocks were originally sited at the north end of the courthouse and moved to their present position, adjacent to the Yeoman's House, in 1904 to commemorate Queen Victoria's Jubilee. The site chosen was that of the old village pound, where stray cattle or sheep were rounded up and kept until their owners paid a fine for their release. A garden was also planted to celebrate the coronation of King Edward VII.

Yeoman's House, *c.* 1930. Another view of this house, numbered 10 Almond's Green (see p.14). The sign on the wall says, 'R. Wearing & Sons, Builders'. Hooper and Simmons now have a garage offering taxis, private cars and weddings.

West Derby village, *c*. 1915. A snowy scene looking from Almond's Green towards the centre of the village.

Village Hall, *c*. 1918. The village hall was built in 1912 and bears the inscription, 'In memory of Hugh McCubbin.' He died in 1911 and lived at Mill Bank House. An alderman on Liverpool Council, he was also a member of the West Derby Local Board. During the Second World War the hall was used as a services canteen and in the 1970s served as Town Row library. It has now been converted into flats.

Church of St Mary the Virgin, c. 1900. Another view of the church, taken from the opposite direction to that on p.9. The clock on the church tower was installed in 1888 in memory of a lady called Anna Maria and is named after her. A sundial on the outer wall of the south transept is dated 1793 and was removed from the old chapel when it was demolished.

St Mary's Church, c. 1975. An atmospheric view of the church, seen from Croxteth Park.

Aerial view of West Derby village, 1921. St Mary's Church can be clearly seen in the centre. The tree-lined drive leads to Croxteth Hall, just visible through the trees in the top right hand corner. Town Row is to the right, with very few buildings, apart from the village hall. The road leading to the centre bottom is Mill Lane and the large house is 'Holly Mount'. The chimneys of West Derby station can just be seen coming into view. The ecclesiastical window above 'Holly Mount' belongs to Crosby Green Methodist church. The large houses of Hayman's Green, can be clearly seen and contrast with the tightly packed housing of The Barracks in the village centre. The nursery to the right of Mill Lane is one of a number in the area. West Derby Cemetery can be seen in the distance across the fields. This photograph highlights the village nature of West Derby at this date and shows how little the surrounding countryside had been developed.

West Derby village, *c.* 1885. The two views of the village centre on this page show how surprisingly little changed in seventy five years. The Monument is still there, of course, and the Yeoman's House. By 1966 the public house on the left, the Hare and Hounds, has been refronted, but the original roof line can still be seen. Even the shop just to the right still appears to have the same frontage.

West Derby village, 1966.

From the tower of St Mary's Church, looking south west, c. 1975. These two views are in striking contrast to the aerial picture of 1921 on p.188. All the surrounding fields have been built on and tower blocks of flats are visible on the horizon.

From the tower of St Mary's Church, looking north, c. 1975. The gardens in the foreground mark the site of West Derby Castle, which had its origins in Saxon times. A motte and bailey castle was later built by the Normans and stood on the site for over 200 years.

Two
The New Estates

Queens Drive, 1930. A block of six houses built by Liverpool Corporation on the Larkhill estate, near Mill Bank.

Larkhill Estate, *c.* 1920. Prior to 1919, Liverpool Corporation had built housing for rent mainly in the city centre. Suburban houses were not built due to the higher costs involved and the problems of transporting people to work. However, after the First World War a general shortage of housing, of all types, led to an expansion of the building programme. Work is just starting here on the Larkhill estate.

Larkhill Lane, *c.* 1925. The majority of the houses on the estate had been completed by 1922. The main criterion for selection for tenancy of municipal housing was ability to pay the rent. This meant that the majority of the tenants were either skilled working class or unskilled workers with steady employment.

Aerial view of the Larkhill Estate, 1922. This is the north end of the estate, with Clubmoor cricket ground in the foreground. Queens Drive runs from left to right across the centre, with Townsend Lane/Townsend Avenue intersecting from top to bottom. The Corporation owned much of the land on the outskirts of the city, including the area bounded by Knowsley Park, Prescot Road and the East Lancashire Road. This had been acquired cheaply, on an ad hoc basis, with the intention of using it for housing. When the photograph was taken approximately 740 houses had been built and practically all were tenanted.

Larkhill Estate, *c.* 1920. The two views here, and that on p.23, give an indication of the variety of architectural styles used on the estate. These houses used redressed stone from the old walls on the estate and the slates have been reused from old buildings.

Walton Park Gardens, 1951. These flats on Queens Drive were built much later than others illustrated here and were not completed until 1950.

Aerial view of Norris Green, *c.* 1930. In the foreground Wapshare Road and Cavan Road form a large loop and immediately above is the Cheshire Lines Railway. In the centre are Circular Road West and Circular Road East, with Broad Square between. Broad Square Infant and Junior Schools can be clearly seen. The wooded area is Norris Green Park, opened in 1933, with Broad Lane beyond.

Townsend Avenue, 1926. Most of the intended 8,000 houses on the Norris Green estate had been built by 1930. Part of the area covered by the estate was outside the Liverpool boundary and did not become part of the city until 1927. All the houses had domestic hot water, electricity and bathrooms. Sites were reserved for public buildings such as churches, libraries, swimming baths and community centres, although not all were built.

Muirhead Avenue, 1937. The Norris Green estate included blocks of flats as well as houses. Flats usually had just one or two bedrooms. The maintenance costs of council housing in 1937 were equivalent to £6.00 per house every year. It was also the intention to decorate each house, internally, every seven years.

Broadway, *c.* 1930. Broadway, near the junction of Townsend Avenue and Utting Avenue, was built as the main shopping centre for the Norris Green estate and the crescent of twenty-five shops was completed in 1929. This busy scene shows the shops shortly after they had opened. However, those on the opposite side of the road have not yet been built. By 1935 there were a total of seventy five shops on the estate.

Broadway, *c.* 1930. A typical selection of shops, with well-known names in the Liverpool area. Waterworth Bros were greengrocers with numerous shops in the suburbs. Blackledges were bakers and Boots Dispensing Chemists are familiar to everyone. Note the delivery bicycle at the kerb. The shop on the right is Bradshaws and has an open front, typical of a fishmongers. Entries in *Kelly's Street Directory* of Liverpool for this date show that there were flats above the shops.

Broadway, 1960. A much later view which shows the opposite side of the road. The Broadway Hall was completed c. 1931 and the roof of the Regal cinema can just be seen to the left. Again the range of shops can be seen and includes a chandler, a hairdresser and a greengrocer and florist.

Almond's Green, *c.* 1935. A block of four 'parlour type' houses on the Norris Green estate. Parlour type houses had a separate parlour and living room and rents were somewhat higher than for non-parlour houses. Typically, rent in 1928, was from 16s 7d (83p) to 19s 6d(97 $\frac{1}{2}$p) for a parlour house, compared with 12s 6d(62$\frac{1}{2}$p) to 14s 4d (72p) for a non-parlour house. The cost of building a parlour house was about £450, compared with £320 to £345 for a non-parlour house.

Glassonby Crescent, 1945. This rebuilt kitchen really is fitted! It has a separate hob and built-in oven, the washing machine is plumbed in and even the fridge is fitted.

Norris Green Restaurant, 1941. During the Second World War Liverpool had the first 'British Restaurants' outside London. These were communal restaurants designed to provide meals for the local community when time for cooking at home was limited. Norris Green Restaurant was in new, purpose built premises. The dining hall seated 280 and, using a self-service system, food was either consumed on the premises or taken home. The restaurant was run using solid fuel to avoid problems with possible interruptions to gas or electicity supplies.

Norris Green Restaurant, interior, 1941. Meals in British Restaurants were provided at breakfast, dinner and supper. Typical menus in 1941, when rationing had been introduced, were: Breakfast: porridge, sausage, baked beans. Dinner: roast beef, carrots, turnips, potatoes, steamed sponge, jam sauce, milk pudding. Supper: sausages in batter, stew, cabbage, potatoes, bread pudding and custard, milk pudding.

Muirhead Avenue East, 1930. Another range of shops, all with uniform frontages: Thomas Tunney, fruit retailers, Irish importers, flowers, fruit, vegetables; Gibson's sweetshop and newsagent, 'Branch of the Chocolate Box', cigarettes, library. (The newspaper placard outside says, 'Latest wires about the Lincoln'); Sayers high class confectioner; Kitchen's, chandlery, hardware (note the display which spills out onto the pavement and up the front of the shop itself); E.J. Thornley, fish, poultry, rabbit salesman; half a dozen rabbits are hanging on the rack, waiting for customers.

Muirhead Avenue, 1925. These three storey buildings are probably flats, as two separate entrances can be seen at the top of the staircase.

Broad Lane area, c. 1925. These houses are still under construction and, even in 1925, small children found building sites attractive play areas.

Scargreen Avenue, *c.* 1933. This shopping centre, known as the Strand, was at the junction of Scargreen Avenue and Utting Avenue East. Benjamin Sykes and Sons Ltd. were principally bakers and had a number of shops in Liverpool. This particular shop, Sykes Cash Stores, was also a grocers, with special offers on margarine, bacon, lemon cheese and eggs.

Deysbrook Lane, 1917. Concrete block house.

Mab Lane, c. 1950. In 1931 Sir Hugo Rutherford, Chairman of the Housing Committee, made the comment that, 'In a very short time our estates will be regarded as some of the most delightful garden cities in the country'. A remark which, unfortunately, did not come true. The Cantril Farm estate was built after the Second World War as building work had been postponed. Work started on the 716 houses and flats in 1946.

Melwood Drive, 1956. Part of this road, running from Town Row to Deysbrook Lane, was built in the mid 1930s. The link was not completed until the 1950s. In the distance construction work is underway on flats opposite Deysbrook Barracks.

Moss Way, Gillmoss, 1981. These modern high rise flats are quite a contrast to the houses, with gardens, which Liverpool City Council built for its tenants in the 1920s and 1930s.

East Lancashire Road, 1928. Here work is underway on building houses and the new East Lancashire Road.

Three
New Roads

Queens Drive, Mill Lane junction, 1948. The semi-detached houses opposite were built on the site of an ancient mill, which was probably destroyed in the early nineteenth century. This is the origin of the road names Mill Lane and Mill Bank. The Jolly Miller public house, on the left, was built on the site of an old tithe barn, also demolished in the ninteenth century. A house called 'Barnfield' was then constructed, only to be demolished for the building of the Jolly Miller. The Bowden Fountain (see p.116) is just out of sight to the right.

Queens Drive, Walton, 1906. Queens Drive was conceived in the early 1900s by John Brodie, the City Engineer of Liverpool. When completed the road provided a seven mile circular route from the north to the south end of the city, avoiding congested areas and passing through what was then undeveloped agricultural land. Here the horse-drawn vehicle is spraying the newly laid road with oil or tar, which was then compacted by the steam roller following behind.

Queens Drive, Walton, 1906. The 'Vet's House' was one of the first buildings to be completed on this stretch of Queens Drive. The vet was Thomas Eaton Jones, MRCVS, the Superintendant of Liverpool Corporation's Veterinary Department and the house was officially named 'Hawkstone'. It was situated close to the Corporation's Walton stables, which were built at about the same time. The house was demolished when Rice Lane flyover was built in the 1960s.

Queens Drive, Walton, 1906. New houses were soon built along Queens Drive, but the rural nature of the area is obvious from this view.

Queens Drive, Walton, 1908. The Vet's House can be seen, with Walton Stables behind, but traffic is so light that the horse and cart can stand in the middle of the road, while the gardener's materials are unloaded. Queens Drive Baths are being built and on the hoarding is a poster for 'Wise's 18/6d suits'.

Queens Drive, Walton, 1922. The public baths have been completed and in 1921 they were used by a total of 121,314 people. Facilities on offer included 1st and 2nd class male and female plunge, 1st, 2nd and 3rd class male and female private baths. Boys under fourteen were charged $\frac{1}{2}$d per person for the open air bath. There was also a public hall.

Queens Drive, Walton, 1922. This is the same junction as shown in the previous view, but looking in the opposite direction.

East Lancashire Road, 1943. The East Lancashire Road, between Manchester and Liverpool, was built to connect the manufacturing areas of East Lancashire with the port and docks of Liverpool. Built at a total cost of £3 million, it was officially opened by King George V in July 1934. *The Daily Express* described it as 'the new wonder road' and it was referred to as a 'super highway'. The Liverpool section, completed in April 1929, had two watering places for steam wagons. More than 2,000 navvies were employed to work on the road and the scale of the project was such that light railways were built to transport the materials.

East Lancashire Road, 1943. This, and the view above, show the junction with Lower House Lane, adjacent to West Derby Cemetery. From the opening of the road there were problems at the junctions. Traffic moved at such speed on the main road, that crossing became hazardous. In an attempt to solve this, a number of traffic islands were built and one is shown here under construction. However, the road retained its reputation as 'dangerous' for many years.

Sugar Brook, 1927. This stream flows parallel to the East Lancashire Road, which can be seen under construction in the distance. It flows into the River Alt adjacent to West Derby sewage farm.

East Lancashire Road, 1938. St Philemon's Church can just be seen to the left, near the junction with Walton Hall Avenue. The arrival of the 44 tram for the Pier Head, via Everton Valley, Scotland Road and Dale Street, has generated a flurry of activity on this cold winter's day.

East Lancashire Road, 1929. An interesting collection of road building equipment. The asphalt mixing machine in the centre is driven by the traction engine on the right. Underneath the machine is a steam driven lorry from the Kirkdale Haulage Co. Ltd. The activity has generated the inevitable audience of men and small boys.

Townsend Avenue, 1927. The houses on the right have been completed and the dual carriageway is in the early stages of construction.

Townsend Avenue, 1928. Six months later the road has been completed and appears to be ready for opening. The notice board on the empty site to the right gives information about shops for rent and other developments. Despite the fact that it is June, the ice cream seller is not doing any trade!

Deysbrook Lane, 1953. A stormwater culvert is under construction and this shows the atrocious conditions in which the men were working, in what must have been a wet December.

Muirhead Avenue, 1924. The tree-lined central reservation of Muirhead Avenue was once part of the drive to Lark Hill House, constructed in the 1880s. The original line can be seen veering to the right in the centre of the picture, with the house hidden in the trees. West Derby Road is in the foreground, with Queens Drive towards the top and the railway beyond.

East Lancashire Road, 1959. This is the bus loading bay at the English Electric factory at leaving off time and this view gives an indication of the large numbers employed there then. The factory was built in 1940/41 for the firm of D. Napier and Son Ltd and acquired by English Electric in 1942. During the war piston engines were built here. In the 1950s a variety of products were made, including switchgear, transformers, washing machines, cookers and the 'large picture television receiver'. Note the prefabs on the opposite side of the road, built after the war to provide temporary housing. English Electric have recently, in 1996, announced that the factory is to close.

Three

Transport

Crown Inn, Leyfield Road, *c.* 1895. This horse-drawn bus is ready and waiting for its passengers. It is possible that the vehicle was built by Hooper and Simmons, carriage builders, who had premises in the the centre of West Derby village from the late 1870s (see p.14).

Horse-drawn tram in the centre of West Derby village, *c.* 1890s. In 1871 plans were drawn up to link all the outlying districts of Liverpool to the city centre by tram. In 1882 the first horse-drawn trams came to West Derby. The terminus was the centre of the village and a two-storey depot was constructed behind the courthouse, shown on the left of the photgraph. Trams were kept on the ground floor and horses had stabling on the first floor, reached via a ramp. Hay was stored on the upper floor.

Horse-drawn tram passing the Sefton Arms, Mill Lane, *c.* 1897. Fares to Liverpool were 4d inside and 3d outside. Trams were painted in different colours depending on their destination. Those to West Derby were green. Note the coat of arms, presumably of the Sefton family, on the building. The Earl of Sefton was the owner of Croxteth Hall.

Two-horse-drawn trams in West Derby village, *c.* 1890s. The advertisements on the trams are for Oldfield's and Nestle's. The tram lines can be seen curving to the left to enter the depot.

Electric tram, *c.* 1900. The track to West Derby was electrified in 1900 and this tram is probably waiting to depart from the Pier Head. By 1914 route number 12 to West Derby via London Road and Church Street was well established. The ordinary service began at 5.05 a.m. from West Derby and its frequency increased to 20 departures an hour. The last car left West Derby at 10.50 p.m. In total there were 212 ordinary departures during the day, with a tram leaving every $2\frac{1}{2}$ minutes during peak times. A level of service which would be envied today.

Electric tram, *c.* 1919. This car has a closed top, in contrast to the previous, earlier, picture. In addition to the ordinary service, first class trams also operated from West Derby. Car number 545 is shown here. The service started somewhat later at 8.30 a.m. and ran four cars per hour.

Electric tram, 1911. This electric tram has been lavishly decorated to celebrate the coronation of King George V on 22 June 1911.

Townsend Avenue, 1928. The number 43 tram has just reached the terminus and its passengers are dispersing. Beyond the Cheshire Lines railway bridge is the Broadway shopping centre. Note the ice-cream seller, with his tricycle, on the left.

Muirhead Avenue, 1924. A tram on route number 29 turns the corner into West Derby Road. The former drive to Lark Hill House which was made into the central reservation of Muirhead Avenue can be seen in the middle. Even the original gateposts have survived.

Mill Bank, 1924. Car number 542, on route 12, waits for its passengers. Note the open cab at the front of the tram, where the driver is exposed to the elements.

Electric tram, 1949. This and the photograph opposite were taken a month before the last trams to West Derby on 21 May 1949. By 1945 there were over 90 miles of tramlines in use in Liverpool and it was possible to travel as far as Stockport or Rochdale, using different operator's trams. However, particularly in a place such as West Derby, with its narrow approach along Mill Lane, the trams caused congestion. They were increasingly seen as obsolete and Liverpool's last tram ran in September 1957.

Electric tram, 1949. This tram, on route number 11, is approaching West Derby village along Mill Lane. The shops on the right are: Brownbills, newsagent; post office (sub-postmistress Ivy Brownbill); James Grundy, cycle dealer; J.H. Dewhurst Ltd, butcher.

Lower House Lane, 1936. An early motor bus on route number 68, which ran from the junction of Queens Drive and Muirhead Avenue to Longmoor Lane, Fazakerley. When the Norris Green estate was built the tramway system was extended along Walton Hall Avenue. A system of buses acting as feeders was set up to take people to the tramway termini for travel to the city centre.

West Derby Station, 1930s. The station, in Mill Lane, was opened in 1884, although the Cheshire Lines Railway had been built through the village in 1879. The line ran from Liverpool, via Edge Hill, then in a loop through West Derby, finishing in Southport.

West Derby Station, 1950. This view was taken shortly after the trams stopped running, although the tracks have not been removed. The station has changed little since the previous photograph. The line closed to passengers in the 1950s and to goods traffic in 1976. It now forms part of a pedestrian and cycle way.

West Derby Station, *c*. 1946. The prize winning station garden. The lady standing is Mrs Allen, who worked at the station as a portress during the Second World War.

Hayman's Green, *c*. 1900. This hearse is bearing at least two coffins, profusely decorated with flowers. Unfortunately the funeral has not been identified.

Walton Stables, 1912. These stables, built for Liverpool Corporation *c.* 1908, were situated adjacent to the Vet's House on Queens Drive (see pp.40, 41). The horse is 'Inkerman'.

Walton Stables, 1924. The concrete construction of the stables can be seen here. The hatbands of the two gentlemen are embroidered 'Liverpool Corporation'.

Four
Around West Derby

Larkhill Lane, 1927. The old and the new. The new Farmer's Arms public house, at the junction of Larkhill Lane and Townsend Lane, replaced an earlier building of the same name. The cottages in front were reputedly built in the fifteenth century.

Larkhill Lane, 1911. This section of Larkhill Lane, adjacent to Lark Hill house, was incorporated into Queens Drive and changed its name.

Queens Drive, 1910. The junction of Queens Drive (formerly Larkhill Lane) and Mill Bank. (see also pp.39, 116). The entrance to Holly Lodge can be seen on the right and Lark Hill is just visible through the trees.

Mill Bank, 1924. Despite the broad dual carriageway there is virtually no traffic. To the left, behind the stone wall, is Mill Bank House.

Eaton Road, c. 1970. Numbers 65 to 71 are late eighteenth or early ninteenth-century cottages built of local sandstone.

Almond's Green, c. 1970. Four stone charity cottages, built in 1863 by J.P. and A.M. Heywood. Their names and the date can be seen on the shield above the doorway.

Almond's Grove, 1939. New, privately built semi-detached houses contrast with the villa on the left.

The Barracks, 1934. This small group of houses situated between Almond's Green and Hayman's Green forms an unexpected contrast with the merchants' villas of West Derby. The origin of the name is unclear, but one suggestion is that a garrison of soldiers was once stationed there. This view shows numbers 23 to 29, which had a very narrow alleyway and high wall at the front of the houses, blocking out most of the light and giving a claustraphobic effect. Note the tin baths and the hand mangle. In 1934 a Housing Committee report recommended that The Barracks should be demolished as they were 'by reason of disrepair or sanitary defects unfit for human habitation'.

The Barracks, 1934. These houses, numbers 18 to 22, have a more open aspect. Typical occupations of the residents in 1911 were: joiner, laundress, labourer, gardener, ostler and cab driver.

The Barracks, 1934. The houses were a mixture of stone and brick built cottages, probably of differing dates. A number have attractive 'Gothic' windows.

Mill Lane, 1949. This view was taken in August shortly after trams stopped running to West Derby, although the single tram track can still be seen. The general appearance is of a pleasant tree-lined country lane.

Mill Lane, 1951. A slightly later view and the road has been resurfaced to cover the tramlines. West Derby station is in the centre and St James's Church just out of the picture to the right.

Eaton Road, 1907. This shop, at the junction of Eaton Road and Mill Lane, is that of M.L. Reichardt, baker, corn dealer and grocer. Note the grain hoist and below it white marks on the wall, presumably from flour as it was unloaded. Martin's (later Barclay's) Bank was built on the left hand corner. The man in uniform is probably a postman.

Eaton Road, c. 1910. From the right the shops are: John R. Williams, fishmonger (on the window it says – fresh fish daily, tripe and cow heels, fried fish, chipped potatoes); David Mitchell, fruit merchant; John Irwin, Sons and Co. Ltd, grocers. Beyond the junction with Norris Green Road is the shop of Edward Boardman, butcher.

Darley Drive, c. 1910. One of a number of roads off Eaton Road which were built in the early 1900s. This road was constructed on the site of a house called Drachenfels, built in 1860 and occupied in 1871 by E. Springman, a general merchant, born in Germany. This postcard is number three in a series of views of West Derby produced by the firm of T.P. & Co.

Bonsall Road, c. 1910. This road runs between Town Row and Eaton Road. St Paul's Roman Catholic church is on the right and the post office, with a group of very well-dressed children, on the left (see p.112).

Apsley Road, 1962. A surprising pocket of undeveloped land in the middle of a housing estate.

Eaton Road, 1965. This photograph appears to show farm buildings. The only farm left in Eaton Road at this date was Beech Farm. The proprietors were James H. Moore and Sons, who were dairymen.

Blackmoor Drive, 1974. This view must have changed little since the houses were built c. 1930. The road takes its name from a house called Blackmoor, whose extensive grounds ran from Eaton Road to Leyfield Road. It was built in 1855 by Philip Jacob Blessig, Russian Consul in Liverpool for fifty years. It was subsequently bought by Rankin Heap, a rice miller, and finally demolished about 1925 (see p.97).

Leyfield Close, off Leyfield Road, 1933. These are newly-built detached houses, each with their own garage. A number of the houses were individually named, straight ahead is Hazeldene.

Leyfield Road, 1893. These old cottages, demolished in 1898, were opposite what is now number 67 Leyfield Road. In the late ninteenth century they were owned by Albert Bencke of 'Olivia' in Eaton Road. The left hand cottage was occupied by the Liderth family and the right hand by the Draycott family. It is possible that they dated from as early as the fifteenth century, with a cruck frame construction and cob walls (see p.14). The gable end has been rebuilt, probably in the eighteenth century, and false timberwork painted on. The original thatched roof has been replaced with Lancashire stone slabs.

Leyfield Road, 1939. These old cottages were situated between Deysbrook Lane and Mayfield Close. In 1939 the white cottage (no.19), with barn attached, was occupied by John Jackson, a cowkeeper.

Tree House, Yew Tree Lane, c. 1900. Yew Tree House was built about 1770 and in 1832 was owned by Lawrence Heyworth, merchant, JP and chairman of the Great Western Railway. He conceived and had built a tree house, complete with staircase, in the branches of an ancient yew tree in the grounds of his house. Afternoon tea was regularly taken there and it was still in existence as late as 1900.

Mab Lane. This postcard has been tentatively identified as Mab Lane, but does not seem to match any of the buildings there. It could be an entrance lodge to Croxteth Park. Can anyone help?

Mab Lane, 1967. These old cottages contrast with the modern housing in the distance. The house at a right angle to the road was once a nursery, with extensive glasshouses at the rear. In 1947 it was run by William E. McFall.

Deysbrook Lane, 1952. Two views of Deysbrook Lane, showing how much of a country lane it was in the early 1950s.

Deysbrook Lane, 1956. This is the junction with Croxteth Hall Avenue, known as Mason's Corner. The wall of Croxteth Park can be seen on the left beyond the junction.

Mercer Place, 1958. Another semi-rural scene, off Deysbrook Lane. Note the unmade road surface.

Deysbrook Lane, 1958. A row of terraced cottages, possibly adjacent to Mercer Place (see previous photograph).

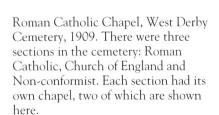

Church of England Chapel, West Derby Cemetery, 1909. In the mid-ninteenth century the population of Liverpool grew rapidly and the churchyards in the city became overcrowded. The Corporation decided to purchase land on the outskirts of the city to open municipally run cemeteries. West Derby Cemetery, situated at the junction of Lower House Lane and the East Lancashire Road opened in 1884.

Roman Catholic Chapel, West Derby Cemetery, 1909. There were three sections in the cemetery: Roman Catholic, Church of England and Non-conformist. Each section had its own chapel, two of which are shown here.

River Alt, near West Derby Sewage Farm, 1951. The sewage farm is situated to the north of the East Lancashire Road. The River Alt eventually flows into the sea at Altcar, south of Formby. In 1895 the Corporation took over the operation of West Derby Sewage Farm. It covered 207 acres and by 1903 dealt with the sewage from 30,000 inhabitants.

River Alt, near West Derby Sewage Farm, 1951. Clock House Farm can be seen behind the trees on the left. Crops grown included rye grass, cabbages, potatoes, mangel-wurzels and beetroot. Income from the produce helped to cover the expense of operating the sewage farm.

Gillmoss, 1921. This poultry farm has not been identified, but the view emphasises the rural nature of the landscape at this time.

St Swithin's Church, Gillmoss, 1944. This is the oldest Roman Catholic church in Liverpool, dating back over 400 years. The mission at Gillmoss derived from the chaplaincy at Croxteth Hall, when the Molyneux family were Catholics. The church shown here was built in 1824. In 1959, with the population of the area increasing, this was replaced by a new, larger building which could accommodate up to 1,000 people.

Five
Hospitals and Schools

Alder Hey Hospital, *c.* 1916. The hospital was used for military personnel during the First World War.

Alder Hey Hospital, 1911. In 1906 the house Alder Hey and its grounds of 28 acres were purchased by the Poor Law Guardians of the West Derby Union, to build a new hospital for sick children. This photograph shows the ceremonial laying of the foundation stone on 30 March 1911. The new hospital was opened in 1914, just at the outbreak of the First World War.

Alder Hey Hospital, c. 1916. Patients, staff and visitors during the First World War, when Alder Hey was used as a military hospital.

Alder Hey Hospital. This group of nurses is undated, but shows the cumbersome uniforms which used to be worn, in contrast to today's more practical outfits.

Alder Hey Hospital, *c.* 1916. View of Ward A2. A postcard published by the Carbonora Company of Wilde Street, Liverpool, a firm which produced a number of topical postcards of Liverpool.

Alder Hey Hospital, 1916. Two patients identified as Lance Corporal F. McLeod of the First Manchester Regiment and Pte.W. Brown of the 2nd Rifle Brigade.

Alder Hey Hospital, 1926. This aerial view gives a good idea of the size of the hospital. In the foreground is Knotty Ash Camp, built during the First World War to accommodate American troops passing through Liverpool. After the war the buildings were purchased by the Corporation and used as temporary housing during the post-war shortage. By 1931 all the huts had been demolished and council houses built on the land.

Norris Green Clinic.

West Derby Church of England School, 1910. A class photograph of Groups V and VI. The pupils included Eddie Riley, Oscar James Brewer and Nat Butler. The headmaster was David James Penton.

West Derby Church of England Primary School, *c.* 1950. The site of the school, in Meadow Lane, was given by the Earl of Derby in 1859, but the cost of the building, £4,985, was raised by public subscription. The school was administered by St Mary's parish church and was originally intended for the education of poorer children. In 1974 a new school was built, but parts of the original building were retained.

West Derby School pupils, 1914.

West Derby School, 1916. Group VI girls.

West Derby School, 1919. Group 6 girls.

West Derby School, c. 1952. Performance of *Snow White and the Seven Dwarfs*.

New Hall Lane School, 1927. This elementary school was situated in Garsfield Road, adjacent to New Hall Lane. Note the wind-up gramophone on the stage.

New Hall Lane School, 1927. A typical classroom of the period. Even the teacher's desk seems somewhat spartan.

LESSONS IN THE SUN. A gardening lesson at the Fazakerley Day Open Air Special School for Delicate Children, Liverpool.

Fazakerley Day Open Air Special School for Delicate Children, 1938. This special school opened in January 1938 and was built almost entirely of glass in order to maximise the benefits of fresh air and sunshine. Accommodation was provided for 300 children and lessons included woodwork, beekeeping and gardening, as shown here.

HOLLY LODGE HIGH SCHOOL, WEST DERBY.

Holly Lodge High School for Girls, *c.* 1930. The house named Holly Lodge was built *c.* 1820 by Isaac Cooke, a Quaker cotton broker and one of the largest landowners in the area. In 1919 the house was purchased by Liverpool Education Committee at a cost of £5,000 and opened as a girls high school in 1922. The neighbouring houses of Sandheys, Fremont and Uplands were later incorporated into the school.

Alsop Comprehensive School, 1982. This school was named after Dr James Wilcox Alsop, chairman of the Education Committee.

Six

Houses

Croxteth Hall, south west view, *c.* 1890. Croxteth Hall was the chief seat of the Earls of Sefton, the Molyneux family. It was acquired in 1473 and continued in the ownership of the family until the 7th Earl died, without an heir, in 1972. It was sold, in lieu of death duties, to Merseyside County Council.

Croxteth Hall, west front, c. 1890. The hall was originally a timber framed building, but has had many additions over the centuries. The west front, shown here, was built during the reign of Queen Anne by the 4th Earl and has the family crest in the centre. The house is now built round a quadrangle, the latest extension in 1902 forming the fourth side. In 1952 a serious fire in the Queen Anne Wing damaged the roof and caused considerable structural damage.

Croxteth Hall, aerial view of the park, 1922. Croxteth Park was laid out by the 3rd Earl in the mid-nineteenth century. In October 1851 Queen Victoria stayed at Croxteth Hall, with Prince Albert and her children, as part of a visit to Liverpool. To the left of the hall, the walled kitchen garden can be seen. This supplied fruit and vegetables for the kitchen and flowers for the house. Even exotic fruit, such as nectarines, could be grown using an ingenious method of heating the walls on which the trees were grown.

Croxteth Hall, 1924. The West Derby Garden Fete, held at Croxteth Hall. On the platform are the Earl and Countess of Sefton, Canon Percy Stewart (the Rector) and Mrs Stewart, Revd George Hodson Foote (the Curate) and Eddie Riley.

Croxteth Hall, 1924. Another view of the garden fete shows the left luggage tent, run by the 23rd Liverpool Company Girl Guides.

Croxteth Hall, c. 1900. This horse-pulled lawnmower shows one way of cutting grass before the invention of motor driven mowers.

Croxteth Park Gates, 1915. This limousine, outside the park gates in West Derby village, was owned by W.E. Hooper. The driver was Tommy Evans.

Croxteth Park, 1978. A view of the mature woodland in the park, near to the park lodge.

Deysbrook, *c.* 1925. This house, in Deysbrook Lane, with its origins in the eighteenth century, was once called Summer Vale. It was renamed Deysbrook in 1847 by the then owner Richard Blundell Hollinshead Blundell, who carried out extensive alterations. The house remained in the family until the early twentieth century, but by 1929 it had become a children's convalescent home. From the Second World War onwards it was used by the army, until demolition in the 1950s. The writer of this postcard was obviously finding West Derby rather quiet, she writes 'nothing fresh in West Derby, in fact it seems quite dead'.

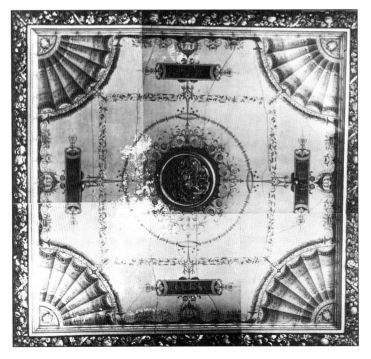

Deysbrook, 1946. As part of the work carried out on the house in the 1840s Richard Blundell Hollinshead Blundell commissioned the artist and sculptor Alfred Stevens to decorate the dining room and two drawing rooms. This is the ceiling of the first drawing room. Stevens decorated and designed furniture, fireplaces and porcelain. He was responsible for the decoration of parts of Dorchester House in London.

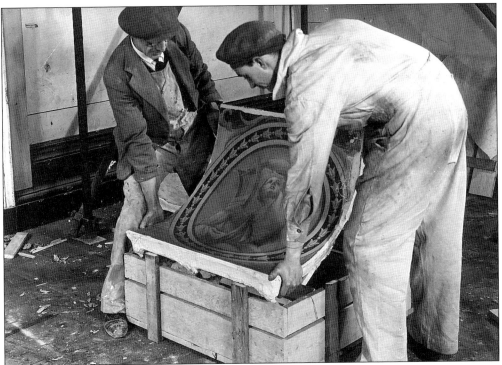

Deysbrook. This undated picture shows the removal of some of the decorative panels from the first drawing room, possibly prior to the demolition of the house. The Walker Art Gallery, Liverpool, has a number of the original murals and many of Stevens drawings.

Blackmoor House, 1926. This house was named after the ancient Blackmoor Moss, a reminder of when the area was just moss and bog. In February 1926 when this photograph was taken work had just started on demolishing the house. Its name was later given to Blackmoor Drive (see p.70).

Sandfield Park East, 1939. These houses lay just off Leyfield Road. Unfortunately one of the gate posts with the end of the name is missing.

Sandfield Park East, 1939. These houses appear to be empty and may be awaiting demolition.

Bradstones, stable block, 1926. This sandstone house in Sandforth Road was built in 1850 by William Lassell, a local brewer and prominent astronomer. In 1927 it became the sports club for the Liverpool department store George Henry Lee. The house and grounds were sold for housing development in 1972 and the house demolished.

Lowlands, Haymans Green, *c.* 1985. This stucco Victorian villa, in its own grounds, was built by Thomas Haigh. It has subsequently been used by the West Derby Community Association.

Lark Hill, c. 1930. This was one of the earlier houses built for Liverpool merchants in the West Derby area. Jonathan Blundell, a colliery owner and merchant, had the house built in 1768. In 1776 it was bought by the Liverpool banker Richard Heywood and it remained in the family until the twentieth century. Liverpool Corporation purchased the building in 1921 and part of it was then used as a branch library. It was demolished in 1962 (see p.119).

Lark Hill, grounds, c. 1930. In the 1880s a grand, tree-lined avenue was laid out to approach Lark Hill from the west. When the Corporation purchased the estate this drive was incorporated as the central reservation of the new Muirhead Avenue (see p.25). However, a sufficient amount of the grounds remained to make the pleasant park shown here.

Fazakerley House, Lower Lane, 1896. This handsome house was reputed to have been owned by the Fazakerley family.

The New Hall, Clubmoor, *c.* 1900. This late seventeenth-century house belonged to the Molyneux family and was demolished in 1926.

Tuebrook (or Tew Brook) House, *c.* 1900. This old sandstone house, now beside the busy dual carriageway at Mill Bank, is thought to have been built in 1615 for John Mercer, a yeoman farmer. It was occupied for many years by Mr Fletcher, a wheelwright, hence the wheels propped up at the front. It is one of Liverpool's oldest houses. In 1921 it was taken over by the Corporation as part of the Larkhill estate and rented as a council house. A 'secret' room in the house is thought to be a priest's hiding hole and it is reputed to have several ghosts.

Seven

People

Deysbrook Football Team, 1923.

Sir William Philip Molyneux, 2nd Earl of Sefton, 1772-1838. The 2nd Earl of Sefton was a keen sportsman and early patron of the Grand National. This print by Richard Dighton was published in 1801 and shows him as 'Lord Dashalong bent on driving', a nickname which apparently stuck.

William Philip Molyneux, 4th Earl of Sefton, 1835-1897. The Molyneux family were descended from Adam de Molineux in the twelfth century. They were influential both as soldiers and noblemen. This, combined with a number of strategic marriages, meant that they owned land stretching from Speke to Altcar. The 4th Earl was responsible for building the major north and east wings of Croxteth Hall.

104

Osbert Cecil Molyneux, 6th Earl of
Sefton, 1871-1930. He married Lady
Helena Mary Bridgeman ('Nellie') in
1898 and they had three children (see
below and following pages).

Children of 6th Earl of Sefton, c. 1905.
Hugh William Osbert (1898-1972) 7th
Earl, Cecil Richard (1899-1916), Evelyn
Mary (1902-1917).

6th Earl of Sefton and his sons, *c.* 1915.
Cecil Richard, here in midshipman's
uniform, was killed at the Battle of Jutland in
May 1916. A memorial service was held at
West Derby church in June 1916.

Revd Andrew McConkey, *c.* 1850. St James
Church, Mill Lane, was built to
accommodate the growing population of
West Derby. The Revd A.W. McConkey was
the first of a number of characterful
clergymen. He was well known in the area
for his donkey and cart, in which he used to
drive himself to church and was, inevitably,
known as 'McConkey's donkey'.

Arthur Heywood. He was responsible for building Norris Green house in 1830. A banker, he was the brother of Richard Heywood of Lark Hill. The house was demolished in 1931 and is now the site of Norris Green park. Arthur Heywood died in 1836 at the age of 83.

John Pemberton Heywood, 1803-1877. He inherited Norris Green from Arthur Heywood. He was an MP, a banker and contributed £4,000 towards the cost of building the tower of St Mary's Church, West Derby. His wife donated the monument which stands in the centre of West Derby village, marking the site of the old chapel of St Mary.

John Alexander Brodie, 1858-1934. J.A. Brodie was City Engineer of Liverpool from 1898 to 1926. A forward thinking man he was responsible for the planning of many of Liverpool's dual carriageway roads. This was in anticipation of increasing traffic, but at a time when traffic was still very light. He was also an inventor. In 1901 he patented a design for the construction of concrete houses and in 1889 for football goal nets. Brodie Avenue is named after him.

St James Church choir, *c.* 1940. The vicar was Canon Harold E. Crewdson, a historian of West Derby and witty writer. The organist was George Galloway.

St James Church. This wedding took place in the 1950s, but the bride and groom have not been identified.

Wedding reception, 1920s. This is the reception of Mr and Mrs Allen, which was held in the garden of Holly Mount. The building in the background is an orchid house.

22 Town Row, *c.* 1915. This house was part of a row of houses called Sefton Terrace. According to *Kelly's Directory* for 1915 the occupant was William Watkinson, a clerk. The elderly woman and child may be relations.

Bessie Braddock, 1946. Bessie Braddock came from humble, militantly left wing origins. She was elected Labour MP for Liverpool Exchange in 1945, with a majority of 637 and became Liverpool's first woman freeman. For many years she lived in Zig Zag Road, off Leyfield Road. At the time of her death, aged 71, in 1970, *The Guardian* described her as 'the best known woman in Britain, after the Queen'.

Children outside L.E. Shillington's shop, 15 December 1951. Shillingtons ran the post office and newsagents, at the junction of Town Row and Bonsall Road, from the late 1920s. The post office is shown in an earlier view (see p.68) and is still there today. The children are well wrapped up on a snowy day, but Father Christmas, in the centre, appears rather wooden. A notice in the shop window invites customers to 'See our Christmas show inside'.

George Bevan Heyworth, 1855-1940. This view, taken *c.* 1920, shows George Bevan Heyworth rowing on the lake behind his house, Fremont, Mill Lane. He was a partner in the firm of Heyworth, Hart and Co., who were produce brokers.

A nun on a tricycle, outside the gates of Croxteth Park, West Derby village.

A piper in West Derby village. Unfortunately the occasion is not recorded.

Black Horse Lane, c. 1912. A haymaking scene. Hay was in demand as horse fodder before the widespread use of the motor car.

Blacksmiths, West Derby, c. 1891. The information which accompanies this photograph states that the blacksmith's forge was in Mill Lane, opposite what is now the chemists. However the only blacksmith, in the late nineteenth century, which the author has been able to trace was John B. Davies, who had premises at 38 and 40 Town Row, between Bonsall Road and Hartington Road.

Bowden Fountain, 1911. This drinking fountain was constructed at the junction of Mill Bank and what was then Larkhill Lane. Thomas Bowden was a gentleman, of 4 Hayman's Green, who died in 1909. The plaque on the fountain says 'Thomas Bowden Fountain erected by his sister 1911.' A similar fountain, at the junction of West Derby Road and Boaler Street, was erected by his daughter in 1913.

Bowden Fountain, 1911. This scene has changed almost beyond recognition (see p.39). Mill Bank, with the tram tracks, is to the left. Larkhill Lane, to the right, was incorporated into Queens Drive and the road widened to form a dual carriageway. The surrounding fields are now housing estates and a pleasant place to sit is now a busy road junction. The fountain is still there, but the lamp at the top is missing.

Eight
Events and Leisure

Rose Queen procession, *c.* 1930. The procession is pictured in Town Row, but the Rose Queen is virtually hidden behind the flowers of her chariot. She is attended by some very solemn pixies or elves.

Regal Cinema, 1955. This cinema, built at Broadway, opened in January 1930 with, appropriately, the film *Broadway Melody*. The first Cinemascope film was shown in March 1955. After a short closure for modernisation, the cinema reopened in October that year with *Such Men are Dangerous*. Halliwell in his film guide describes the film as 'totally unmemorable'! The cinema closed in 1964 and is now a bingo hall.

Regal Cinema, interior, 1955. The Regal was the first specifically built 'talkie' cinema in Liverpool. It incorporated a stage and a suite of dressing rooms, intended for variety acts.

Larkhill Library, 1939. A branch library was opened in part of Lark Hill, Queens Drive, in December 1928. The rest of the house was used as a community centre. (see p.100). The building was demolished in 1962 after being found to have extensive dry rot.

Larkhill Library, c. 1930. This interior view shows how the rooms of the house have been adapted for use as a library. Note the moulded ceiling. The picture on the wall is probably an old view of the house.

Larkhill Library, July 1964. This view of the new Larkhill library makes an interesting contrast sith the previous photograph. The style and fittings are typical of the 1960s.

Norris Green Library, 1938. This library, officially named the Henry A. Cole Branch Library, after the chairman of the Libraries, Museums and Arts Committee, was opened on 12 October 1937. The building cost £12,750 and occupies a site of 3,200 square yards adjacent to the Broadway shopping centre.

Norris Green Library, c. 1931. Before the new library was opened Norris Green had been provided with a temporary library, at a cost of £1,067. Although the premises were small, it was obviously well patronised, with loans of about 10,000 each week in 1931-32.

Norris Green Library, 1937. A brand new library, with all the books tidy, waiting for opening. There was a lending library for adults and for young people, also a general reading room. This view is of the lending library.

Norris Green Library, the Lending Library for Young People, 1937. Note the glass screen at the counter separating staff and readers. The magazines available are: *Boy's Own*, *Girl's Own*, *Meccano Magazine*, *Scout* and *The Children's Newspaper*.

West Derby War Memorial, 1921. The war memorial, recording the names of local men who died in the First World War, was unveiled in June 1921. The unveiling obviously attracted a large crowd.

West Derby War Memorial, June 1921. Another view of the unveiling ceremony.

West Derby village, 1952. Soldiers, possibly from the Liverpool Scottish Regiment, marching through the village on Remembrance Day, 9 November 1952. They are reviewed by the Earl of Sefton and Canon Frank Jones, rector of St Mary's Church.

West Derby Flower Show, 1927. The ladies are dressed in their best and the carefully carried cake is a centre of attention.

Liverpool Boys Association Incorporated playing fields, (Walker Ground), Leyfield Road, c. 1951.

Cunard Sports Ground, Bellefield, 1932. The original Bellefield house was built, in mock gothic style, c. 1820, for Mr Spencer Jones, an iron founder. In 1871 the house was bought by Sir Edward (Bully) Bates, a ship owner and East India merchant. He acquired a poor reputation locally through overloading his ships, leading to loss of life. The house remained unoccupied for many years, but in 1920 the grounds were used as the Cunard Sports Club. After the Second World War it became Everton Football Club's training ground.

Walker Playing Fields, 1949.

Melwood, 1955. This is now Liverpool Football Club's training ground. Originally a farm field, it became the sport's field for St Francis Xavier's College in about 1920 and was acquired by the football club in 1951.

Dog & Gun Inn, 1927. This public house gave its name to a school, a post office and a village. It was situated in Carr Lane and in 1927 the licensee was Philip Maher.

Crown Inn, Leyfield Road, 1939. A new public house has replaced the building seen on p.49.

Acknowledgements

The author would like to thank those members of the West Derby Society
who have allowed their photographs to be reproduced in this book and in particular
Mrs Frankla Corris for her assistance.
I would also like to thank David Stoker, Manager of the Liverpool Record Office
and staff of Liverpool Libraries and Information Services.